21st Century
SKILLS LIBRARY

PRESIDENTIAL DEBATES

T0062335

by
Samantha
Bell

CHERRY LAKE PRESS

CHERRY LAKE PRESS

Published in the United States of America by
Cherry Lake Publishing Group
Ann Arbor, Michigan
www.cherrylakepublishing.com

Reading Adviser: Beth Walker Gambro, MS, Ed., Reading Consultant, Yorkville, IL

Content Editor: Mark Richards, Ph.D., Professor, Dept. of Political Science,
Grand Valley State University, Allendale, MI

Photo Credits: © AP Photo/Jeff Roberson, cover, title page; New York World-Telegram
& Sun Collection, Library of Congress, Prints and Photographs Division, 5; United Press
International, Public domain, via Wikimedia Commons, 7; Cecil Stoughton, White House,
Public domain, via Wikimedia Commons, 8; Series: Reagan White House Photographs,
1/20/1981 - 1/20/1989Collection: White House Photographic Collection, 1/20/1981
- 1/20/1989, Public domain, via Wikimedia Commons, 10; Gage Skidmore from Peoria,
AZ, United States of America, CC BY-SA 2.0, via Wikimedia Commons, © Andrew
Cline/Shutterstock, 13; © DFree/Shutterstock, 14; © Stacey Newman/Shutterstock,
15; George Bush Presidential Library and Museum, Public domain, 17; Pete Souza,
Public domain, via Wikimedia Commons, 18; © Joseph Sohm/Shutterstock, 19;
Official Navy Page from United States of AmericaMCSN Declan Barnes/U.S. Navy,
Public domain, via Wikimedia Commons, 21; David Hume Kennerly, Public domain, via
Wikimedia Commons, 23; freddthompson, CC BY-SA 2.0 via Wikimedia Commons, 25;
© DC Studio/Shutterstock, 26; © Joseph Sohm/Shutterstock, 29; Matt Lemmon, CC
BY-SA 2.0, via Wikimedia Commons, 30; Another Believer, CC BY-SA 3.0, via Wikimedia
Commons, 31; © Mike_shots/Shutterstock, 33; © igor moskalenko/Shutterstock, 34;
Richard Nixon Presidential Library, Public domain, via Wikimedia Commons, 37; George
Bush Presidential Library and Museum, Public domain, 39; George Bush Presidential
Library and Museum, Public domain, 40; George Bush Presidential Library and
Museum, Public domain, 41; © Joseph Sohm/Shutterstock, 42; Jimmy Carter Library,
Public domain, 43

Cherry Lake Press is an imprint of Cherry Lake Publishing Group.

Library of Congress Cataloging-in-Publication Data has been filed and is available at
catalog.loc.gov

Printed in the United States of America

Note from Publisher: Websites change regularly, and their future contents are outside of our control.
Supervise children when conducting any recommended online searches for extended learning opportunities.

CONTENTS

CHAPTER 1

THE PURPOSE OF DEBATES

Candidates running for president will often take part in debates. A debate is a discussion about the issues. A **moderator** asks the candidates questions. The questions may be about their platforms. They may be about the candidates' experience. They may be about something they said. The candidates then have a set amount of time to answer.

Debates are often held before the primaries. Some or all of the party's candidates might take part in the debates. Some candidates may not qualify to join. They may not have enough support. The other candidates can choose whether they want to join or not.

After the party conventions, the nominees from each party can debate each other. These debates

N.Y. COUNTY *Welcomes*

TOM DEWEY
OUR
NEXT PRESIDENT

WELCOME
· TO QUEENS ·
Our Next PRESIDENT
Thomas E. Dewey

Thomas Dewey during his 1948 presidential campaign

usually include only the candidates from the Republican and Democratic parties. Third-party candidates are not usually invited.

REACHING MILLIONS

One of the earliest presidential debates occurred before the Oregon Republican primary in 1948. Thomas Dewey and Harold Stassen participated. The race was very close.

The debate was **broadcast** over the radio. Forty million people listened. They heard it live as it was happening. The debate covered just one issue. Each man had 20 minutes to speak. Dewey was a lawyer. He was very good at making a case for his viewpoint. He was the clear winner. He went on to win the primary. He became the party's nominee.

In the 1950s, television was a new technology. It caught on quickly with Americans. In 1949, only 172,000 television sets had been sold. By 1953, the number had risen to more than 52 million. Candidates had to deal with this new type of media.

There were four televised presidential debates in 1960.

They had to figure out how to present themselves and their policies to the voters.

By 1960, television had become the main media source. That year, the first debate between party nominees took place on TV. Democrat John F. Kennedy went face-to-face with Republican Richard Nixon. Nixon had served as vice president for 8 years. He was much better known than Kennedy.

Sixty-five million people watched the debate. The voters could see the candidates. Kennedy looked young and confident. He was tan from campaigning outdoors.

John. F. Kennedy (1917–1963) was the president of the
United States from 1961 to 1963.

Nixon appeared pale and sweaty. He had been in the hospital and looked tired. Some people said Nixon won on the radio. But Kennedy won on TV.

Kennedy went on to win the presidency. People began to understand the importance of the debates. They could boost candidates who performed well. Candidates who did poorly could lose support.

INFORMING THE PEOPLE

An election year usually has several debates. The most important is the first debate. The voters don't know as much about the candidates. More voters are undecided.

Debates give voters an opportunity to see a candidate in action for more than just a few minutes. They learn how the candidates stand on the issues. They listen to the candidates' opinions. They think about what candidates say. They see how the candidates respond to tough questions.

Ronald Reagan in a presidential debate against Walter Mondale, 1984's Democratic candidate

Voters also watch how candidates behave. A candidate's personality often comes out during a debate. People can often get a sense of the candidate's willingness to listen. They can see if a candidate is **mean-spirited** or sincere. A debate gives the voters a chance to get to know more about the candidate's character.

For example, Ronald Reagan often used humor during debates. In a 1984 debate, a moderator asked a question about his age. Reagan answered with a joke. Even his opponent laughed. It clinched Reagan's popularity with the voters. It didn't seem to matter that he sometimes got facts wrong. He won the election by a landslide.

TRUE STORY: **FIRST LADY, FIRST DEBATE**

In 1956, President Dwight Eisenhower was running for reelection. His opponent, Adlai Stevenson, challenged him to a debate. But two substitutes debated the issues instead. Former **First Lady** Eleanor Roosevelt represented Stevenson and the Democrats. Senator Margaret Chase Smith represented Eisenhower and the Republicans. It was the first televised presidential debate between the two parties.

Roosevelt was a great speaker. But Smith had a strategy. She carefully chose her clothes and hairstyle. She answered the questions politely and briefly. She let Roosevelt have more time to talk. But in the last 2 minutes, Smith was forceful. She addressed many key issues. Roosevelt was angry. She would not even shake Smith's hand. Eisenhower later won the election.

CHAPTER 2

DEBATE FORMATS

The debates between Kennedy and Nixon showed the importance of image. During the next three presidential elections, some of the candidates decided that a debate would hurt their campaigns. They didn't participate in any debates. In 1976, the League of Women Voters brought back the debates. Candidates have been debating ever since. Today, most presidential debates are run by the Commission on Presidential Debates (CPD).

The CPD makes sure that debates are held before the general election. It **sponsors** the debates. It raises its own funds from communities, businesses, and individuals. The CPD also organizes the debates. It decides how many debates there will be that year. It establishes the guidelines.

Libertarian candidate Gary Johnson didn't have enough voter support to participate in the 2016 presidential debates.

Candidates must meet certain requirements if they want to join a CPD debate. They must have enough support to get on the ballot. They must also have support from at least 15 percent of the country's voters.

Newspapers, magazines, and nonprofit organizations can also sponsor debates. They determine the format and guidelines. Candidates may suggest debates. They may be confident in their abilities. Or they may be behind in the **polls**. If they do well, a debate could help them gain an edge over a competitor.

Journalist Chris Wallace moderated presidential debates in 2016 and 2020.

EARLY DEBATES

The format of the debates has changed over the years. In the first debate, Kennedy and Nixon sat at tables, but spoke behind a podium when it was their turn. The moderator sat at a table. The moderator asked the questions. The candidates took turns answering.

Beginning in 1976, the debates had a different format. Each candidate stood behind a podium. The moderator explained the rules. They kept the debate moving along. This time, a panel of three **journalists** asked the questions.

The moderators and panelists were mostly high-ranking journalists from television and radio.

Anderson Cooper was a
moderator for the 2016
U.S. presidential debates.

There were no time limits on how long they could speak. The campaigns often argued about who the moderators would be.

By the 1980s, the debates seemed more like **press conferences**. Some people thought the moderators took up too much time. They took attention away from the candidates.

Today, debates have one or more moderators. A good moderator should keep track of the time. Their job is to make sure the candidates are participating. They try to make the debate as fair and interesting as possible.

TIME FOR A CHANGE

In 1987, the CPD took over. It wanted to focus on the candidates and their views. Its first set of debates used one moderator with a panel of three journalists. But in 1992, it tried a different format. That year, Democratic candidate Bill Clinton held many small meetings before the primaries in New Hampshire.

Bill Clinton spoke with voters at a 1992 town hall presidential debate.

He met with voters and answered their questions. He called these "town hall meetings." They were so successful that Clinton suggested a town hall debate.

The CPD agreed. Along with two traditional debates, a town hall debate was also held. The town hall format has been used in every election since then. The meetings are made up of approximately 100 undecided voters. They may live in the area where the debate takes place. Sometimes they are flown in from other parts of the country. The important thing is that

Barack Obama preparing for a presidential debate in 2012

they are not journalists. They are regular people with real concerns.

In 2012 and 2016, the CPD tried another format with the traditional debates. One of the debates focused only on foreign policy. The other focused only on domestic issues. Each of these debates was divided into segments. The segments were 15 minutes long. Each segment focused on one major issue.

The moderators chose the topics for the segments. Topics were announced several weeks before the debate. That way, the candidates would have time to prepare. Some people hoped this format would encourage meaningful discussion of the issues.

FUN FACT: THE MUTE BUTTON

In 2020, Joe Biden ran for president against Donald Trump. During their first debate, Trump kept interrupting Biden as he tried to answer questions. This led to the candidates talking over each other throughout the debate. For the next debate, organizers added a mute button. The moderator muted the candidates' microphones when it was not their turn to speak.

CHAPTER 3

MEDIA

Media refers to many types of communication formats. These include TV, newspapers, and radio. Media also includes the internet and streaming platforms. *The media* is a term people use that includes any or all of these formats. It is important to remember that the media includes a wide range of sources and viewpoints.

People turn to the media for news. They expect the media to cover important political events. This helps them make more informed decisions.

Getting information from the media wasn't always easy. During most of U.S. history, people didn't have televisions. They had to find out about the candidates through speeches and letters. They learned about the political conventions from newspaper articles.

Today, people can watch the debates as they are happening. They can also watch online on streaming

People around the world can watch the U.S. presidential debates, including deployed service members in the U.S. Armed Forces.

platforms. If they miss a debate, they can watch it anytime online.

WIN OR LOSE

The media has a strong influence on how voters view a debate. This depends on how the media approaches it. One way is called a policy frame. In this approach, the media discusses the issues presented during the debate. They talk about the candidates and their policies. This type of coverage can help voters make decisions. The voters can focus on the important topics that were discussed. They can decide about the candidates and their platforms.

Another approach is the game frame. This is when the media views the debate as a competition. They cover the debate like a sports event. They emphasize who won and who lost. They talk about who looked the best. They analyze each candidate's **body language**. They discuss how well the candidates connected with the voters.

This type of coverage can lessen the value of the debates. When the media treats a debate like a competition, viewers think less about the issues. They tend to focus on what the media focuses on. The debate is not as useful for helping them make informed decisions.

An example of this is a 1976 debate between Gerald Ford and Jimmy Carter. Near the end of the debate, Ford **misspoke**. He meant to say that the **Soviet Union** didn't have as much control over other countries as it claimed. Instead, he said there was no Soviet control of these countries.

What Ford said was incorrect. Polls were taken right after the debate. They showed that viewers were not worried about the mistake. They didn't think it

Gerald Ford misspoke during this debate. Debates can shape how people view the candidates. Jimmy Carter went on to win the 1976 presidential election.

was that important. Many viewers thought Ford "won" the debate. There is not an official winner in a presidential debate. But many viewers thought Ford did the best job.

But many journalists saw it differently. They said Ford's statement was a huge mistake. They said it made him lose the debate. The next day, Ford had a press conference. Journalists tried to get Ford to say he had messed up. The media continued to focus on it the next day as well. Soon, many of the same viewers thought Ford lost the debate.

SPIN ROOMS

The term *spin* refers to a certain way people use words and images to describe events. It is when people try to make themselves or their political party look good. Campaigns try to spin the results of debates. They want people to think their candidate won.

After a debate, the candidates meet with reporters to answer questions. These unofficial meetings are called spin rooms. They aren't actual rooms. But they are places where candidates can spin their performance in the debate.

In the spin rooms, reporters ask the candidates follow-up questions. They want to know more about the issues discussed during the debate. These spin sessions can sometimes provide more information. During a debate, the candidates have a limited amount of time to speak. They can freely talk in the spin rooms.

The candidates are not the only ones spinning. Members of their campaign team also spin the debate. So do their supporters. Even if the

Many interviews happen in the spin rooms following presidential debates. People are asked their opinions on the debate.

Anyone can fact-check what the candidates are saying in debates. It is very important. Look at reliable sources to fact-check.

candidate doesn't do as well, the team usually says they did the best. With social media, people can spin anywhere and anytime. And it is not just the candidates and their teams. Anyone can spin as the debate is going on.

SPOTLIGHT ON: FACT-CHECKERS

Fact-checkers pay attention to the candidates and what they say. They make sure what the candidates are saying is true. This includes posts on social media. It includes statements made in ads. It also includes remarks they make during the debates. If something is false, they publish it online. That way, people will know.

Sometimes the moderator is a fact-checker too. The candidates answer the questions. Then the moderator checks to see if what they say is true. If not, they may ask a follow-up question. Sometimes the fact-checkers are reporters. They ask follow-up questions after the debate.

CHAPTER 4

SOCIAL MEDIA WEIGHS IN

Today, Americans can get their news from lots of media sources. Many get their news from social media. These include platforms like Facebook, X, and YouTube. They also include Instagram and TikTok.

Social media can help both candidates and voters. It can get a candidate's message out. Social media can communicate with voters directly. It can also help voters decide which candidates to support.

Social media has become a part of the presidential debates too. People get on social media before, during, and after the debates. They use the platforms to talk about the candidates. They can discuss the issues in real time.

THE DEBATE MOVES ONLINE

Barack Obama was the first presidential candidate to use social media. In 2008, Obama used it to rally his

Because of social media, voters were able to follow Obama's 2008 campaign more closely. He went on to win the presidency. He won again in 2012.

supporters and win votes. His campaign had accounts on several social media platforms. These platforms allowed Obama to reach all types of voters. The campaign shared speeches, photos, and interviews on social media. They encouraged people to share their own stories and thoughts.

The impact of social media continued to grow during the 2016 election. Hillary Clinton was the Democratic candidate. Donald Trump ran for the Republicans. Both campaigns posted messages and

Many people gathered together to watch the 2016 presidential debates on television and online.

photos on social media. When it was time for the debates, platforms such as YouTube and Twitter (now X) streamed them live. The first debate drew the most viewers in U.S. history. Eighty-four million people watched it on television. Millions more watched online.

During the debates, the campaign teams connected with voters on social media. They wanted to energize their supporters. They posted quotes and graphics. They worked to help their candidate get more attention. They also wanted to make their opponents look bad. They used social media to criticize their answers to the debate questions.

The campaign teams were not the only ones to use social media. More than 17 million tweets were sent on Twitter during the debate. Nearly 31 million election-related tweets were sent throughout the day. They included many attacks on the candidates. They came from the public, the campaigns, and the candidates themselves.

Later debates followed this early trend. Users still go on social media to share their thoughts and reactions. They discuss the topics and interesting moments. Campaigns join in to share their views of the debates. But it can be difficult to keep the discussion helpful and positive.

MISINFORMATION AND DISINFORMATION

Misinformation is false or inaccurate information. It may be rumors about the candidates. It could be a false statement about an issue. Disinformation is false information that is meant to deceive someone.

Anyone can spread misinformation and disinformation on social media.

In politics, it is used to mislead voters. Both misinformation and disinformation are common during elections.

Information spreads very quickly on social media. After a debate, people go to social media to talk about it. Campaign teams try to build up their candidate as the winner. Voters show their support or give their reactions. Experts analyze what the candidates said.

But some of the posts are misinformation and disinformation. Statements can be taken out of context. They may even be outright lies. Videos may have been edited. They may show something different than what actually happened.

Make sure to verify that what you're watching online is actually true.

Some videos are called deepfakes. These are videos created by artificial intelligence (AI) programs. They appear real. People may hear a candidate say something. But it could be completely fake. These videos can fool people into believing something that is not true.

Voters need to guard themselves against misinformation and disinformation. The best way is to watch the debates themselves. That way, voters can make their own judgments. They don't have to depend on what someone tells them. They can also use other sources to **verify** what they see on social media.

PERSPECTIVES: DEBATING ONLINE

In 2016, Donald Trump and Hillary Clinton prepared for their first debate. Third-party candidates were also running against them. They included Jill Stein of the Green Party and Gary Johnson of the Libertarian Party. They wanted to participate in the debates too. They believed all four candidates should be included.

But Stein and Johnson didn't have enough voter support to join in the debate. They needed to reach an average of 15 percent support in the national polls. So the candidates and their supporters took to social media instead. They used it to protest the debate. They also used it to discuss their views on the issues during the debate.

CHAPTER 5

THE IMPACT OF DEBATES

Debates offer candidates a great opportunity. Through TV and the internet, they can reach millions of people at once. Voters are tuned in and listening. Candidates may be able to connect with the voters. This can improve their chances of winning.

Debates offer candidates a way to share where they stand on the issues. People can get to know the candidates better. Debates can help voters decide who to vote for.

FROM UNDECIDED TO DECIDED

Undecided voters watch debates to hear the candidates' views. They listen to see which views match their own. They also pay attention to the candidates' personalities. They decide if a candidate would make a good president.

After John. F. Kennedy won the presidential election in 1960, he met with then Vice President Nixon to discuss the changes that would be taking place. Without the debates, Kennedy may not have become president.

Debates also give voters the chance to compare candidates. They can see and hear the candidates side by side. In the 1960 debate, people noticed how Kennedy and Nixon looked. But they also noticed something else. Nixon had served as U.S. vice president. He had a lot more experience. But on stage together, Nixon and Kennedy looked more like equals. People began to view Kennedy as a potential president.

Debates also help bring attention to candidates who are not as well-known. In 1992, Ross Perot ran as an independent. He was invited to join the debates. As a third party candidate, he didn't have much of a chance to win the election. But the debate brought him more supporters. Before the debate, the polls showed him with 7 percent of the vote. By election day, he was up to 19 percent. Some experts believe this increase was a result of the debates.

Reporters who cover debates often look for a winner and loser. But voters experience debates differently. They want to understand what the candidates think of the issues. They want to figure out which candidate is the best choice.

Ross Perot speaking at the 1992 town hall presidential debate

MAKE IT OR BREAK IT

Doing well in a debate can benefit a campaign. It can help boost a candidate's image. It can also help them win votes. Bill Clinton took part in the first town hall debate. He practiced for the debate. He worked on his body language. He planned where he would be on stage. The debate helped him become more likable. Many people believe this helped him win the election.

A 1992 presidential town hall debate

Appearances are very important in presidential debates. A candidate needs to think about how things will look to the audience.

Debates are not easy for the candidates. They are under a lot of pressure to perform well. They must think quickly. They must try not to say something incorrectly or make a wrong move. For example, in 1992, an audience member asked President George H. W. Bush a question. She wanted to know how the **national debt** affected him. At the exact same time, he checked his watch. People thought he didn't care. But he just wanted the debate to be over.

These types of simple actions can make a candidate look bad. In the 1960 debate, Nixon would sometimes look off to the side. He was looking at the reporters.

Al Gore lost the 2000 presidential election to George W. Bush.

But it made him appear like he had shifty eyes. He seemed like he could not be trusted. In 2000, people could hear Al Gore sighing during the debate. It sounded as if he was bored.

Debates are part of a campaign's strategy. The candidates don't have to take part in the debates. They are not required. Instead, candidates must decide if participating could help or hurt their campaign.

FUN FACTS: THE MOST FAMOUS MICROPHONE

Ronald Reagan was a candidate in the 1980 election. He paid the expenses for one of the primary debates. At the beginning of the debate, he tried to make an announcement. The moderator didn't want him to speak. He tried to have Reagan's microphone cut off. Reagan told him he was paying for the microphone. People cheered. They saw Reagan as being firm and fair.

ACTIVITY

TAKE A STAND

During a debate, candidates let voters know where they stand on the issues. You and your friends or family can practice taking a stand on issues too.

First, gather several friends or family members to come take a stand!

Next, cut a piece of paper into six strips. On each strip, write one of the following statements:
- Students should be allowed to have cell phones in school.
- Students should not have homework over the weekend.
- Students should not have to take standardized tests.
- Screen time should be limited to a certain number of hours a day.
- Students younger than age 16 should have a bedtime.
- Schools should be required to serve healthy lunches and snacks.

Flip the papers upside down. Then have someone choose one of the papers and read the statement aloud.

Go around the group and find out if they agree or disagree with the statement. Have them give a reason why they think that way. After everyone has had a chance to speak, ask if anyone has changed their mind after listening to the other opinions. On another sheet of paper, record:
• The statement
• The number of people who agreed at first
• The number of people who disagreed at first
• The number of people who changed their minds

Continue in the same way with the rest of the statements. Did any of the results surprise you? Why or why not?

GLOSSARY

body language (BAH-dee LANG-gwij) communication expressed through gestures, facial expressions, and posture instead of words

broadcast (BRAWD-kast) transmitting a message, program, or information through radio or television to a large audience

first lady (FURST LAY-dee) the wife of the president of the United States

journalists (JUR-nuh-lists) professionals who gather, analyze, and present news and information to the public through various media outlets

mean-spirited (MEEN SPEER-uh-tuhd) behavior or actions that are unkind or intended to cause harm or distress to others

misspoke (mihs-SPOHK) spoken inaccurately, usually by mistake

moderator (MAH-duh-ray-tuhr) person who presides over a debate

national debt (NA-shuh-nuhl DET) the amount of money a federal government owes

polls (POHLZ) surveys or questionnaires for gathering public opinion on political candidates, issues, or policies

press conference (PRES KAHN-fruhns) a meeting where a public figure speaks to the media, makes announcements, and answers questions

sponsors (SPAHN-suhrz) people or groups who financially support and organize an event

Soviet Union (SOH-vee-et YOON-yuhn) a former country (1922–1991) that extended from eastern Europe to northern Asia

verify (VER-uh-fye) to confirm the accuracy or truth of something by investigating or finding evidence

TO LEARN MORE

BOOKS

Brown, Robin Terry. *Breaking the News: What's Real, What's Not, and Why the Difference Matters*. Washington, D.C.: National Geographic Kids, 2020

Burgan, Michael. *TV Shapes Presidential Politics in the Kennedy-Nixon Debates*. North Mankato, MN: Compass Point Books, 2019.

Corso, Phil. *Presidential Debates*. New York: PowerKids Press, 2019.

WEBSITES

Search these online sources with an adult:

"How Does the Media Shape Political Opinions?" PBS.

"What Would a Better Format for the Presidential Debates Look Like?" NBC News.

"Your Guide to Mis- and Disinformation." League of Women Voters' Education Fund.

INDEX

ABOUT THE AUTHOR

Samantha Bell was born and raised near Orlando, Florida. She grew up in a family of eight kids and all kinds of pets, including goats, chickens, cats, dogs, rabbits, horses, parakeets, hamsters, guinea pigs, a monkey, a raccoon, and a coatimundi. She now lives with her family in the foothills of the Blue Ridge Mountains, where she enjoys hiking, painting, and snuggling with their cats, Pocket, Pebble, and Mr. Tree-Tree Triggers.